What Believers Must Know to Grow

Tom Carter's treatment of this message to new Christians is not merely another book on the topic of what such individuals must know and do to grow into spiritual maturity. It is personally and refreshingly written in such a way as to make simple and viable what so many tend to present as complex and out of reach for most.

Donald E. McClean, Brookings, OR

I've been a Christian since my childhood and I thought once I invited Christ into my heart, my part was done. It took me several years of stumbling around in the dark before I understood that my life as a Christian was lacking in maturity and growth. I wish I had read this book years ago!

Christine Miller, Dinuba, CA

This is a clear, practical, hands-on guide that may be intended for young believers but reminds mature disciples, as well, of God's standard for everyday Christian living.

Holly Gordon, Clifton Park, NY

In this book, Dr. Carter answers the real questions new Christians ask. His answers are true to life, crisp, and biblical.

Dr. Al Machiela, Kennewick, WA

WHAT BELIEVERS MUST KNOW TO GROW

TOM CARTER

Other books by Tom Carter:

Cover to Cover: A Devotional Survey of Every Book in the Bible

For Members Only: A Guide to Responsible Church Membership

Promises by the Dozen

Spurgeon at His Best

Evangelical Jargon: A Glossary of Christian Words and Terms

What Believers Must Know to Grow

Tom Carter

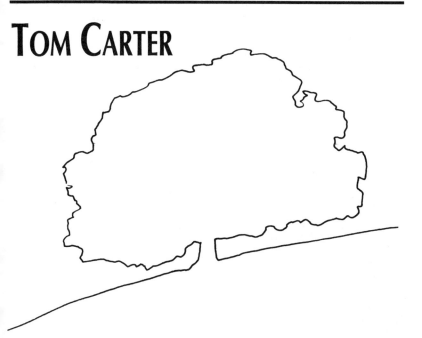

Evergreen Communications, Inc.
Ventura, California

WHAT BELIEVERS MUST KNOW TO GROW

Published by
Evergreen Communications, Inc.
2085-A Sperry Avenue
Ventura, CA 93003
(805) 650-9248

Unless otherwise indicated, Scripture quotations are from the *New American Standard Bible*, © The Lockman Foundation 1960, 1962, 1963, 1968, 1971, 1972, 1973, 1975, 1977. Used by permission.

Other versions used include:

KJV—King James Version.

NIV—From the *Holy Bible, New International Version.* © 1973, 1978, 1984 International Bible Society. Used by permission of Zondervan Bible Publishers.

RSV—From *Revised Standard Version* of the Bible, copyrighted 1946 and 1952 by the Division of Christian Education of the NCCC, U.S.A.

TLB—Scripture verses are taken from *The Living Bible* © 1971 owned by assignment by Illinois Regional Bank N.A. (as trustee). Used by permission of Tyndale House Publishers, Inc., Wheaton, IL 60189. All rights reserved.

Library of Congress Cataloging-in-Publication Data:
Carter, Tom, 1950—
   What believers must know to grow / Tom Carter.
      p.   cm.
   ISBN 0-926284-01-0
   1. Christian life—1960—   I. Title
BV4501.2.C273   1990   90-47407
248.4—dc20   CIP

99 98 97 96 95 94 93 92 91 90   9 8 7 6 5 4 3 2 1

Printed in the United States of America

The author and publisher have sought to locate and secure permission to reprint copyrighted material in this book. If any such acknowledgments have been inadvertently omitted, the publisher would appreciate receiving the information so that proper credit may be given in future printings.

To

Helen Day Carter

my mother

who taught me to love Christ when I was three years old,
trained me in the way I should go (Proverbs 22:6),
and set the example for me to follow.

Contents

One

What's So Important About Spiritual Growth?

13

Two

Can I Be Sure of My Salvation?

17

Three

When Does God Get Even?

25

Four

Why Am I Here?

33

Five

What Do You Mean, Fifteen Minutes a Day Will Change My Life?

41

Six

I Tried to Live for Christ, But It Didn't Work

49

Seven

Why Do I Feel Like a Walking Civil War?

57

Eight

Aren't All Christians the Same?

65

Nine

What's the Difference Between Temptation and Sin?

73

Ten

Why Do My Prayers Seem to Bounce off the Ceiling?

81

Eleven

I Can Worship God at the Beach...Can't I?

91

Twelve

Do I Have to Be Committed?

99

A One-Year Plan for Bible Verse Memorization

105

One

What's So Important About Spiritual Growth?

Grow in the grace and knowledge
of our Lord and Savior Jesus Christ.
2 Peter 3:18

This book is written for young believers in Christ. If you have recently invited Jesus into your heart as personal Savior, congratulations! Welcome to the family of God.

Perhaps you've been a Christian for years, but you know you haven't grown spiritually. Then you, too, can profit from the pages ahead.

Many Christians wonder, *What's so important about spiritual growth?* I'll let the Bible answer that question:

- "Grow up in all *aspects* into Him, who is the head, *even* Christ" (Ephesians 4:15).
- "Your faith is greatly enlarged, and the love of each one of you toward one another grows *ever* greater" (2 Thessalonians 1:3).
- "Let us press on to maturity" (Hebrews 6:1).
- "Grow in respect to salvation" (1 Peter 2:2).
- "Grow in the grace and knowledge of our Lord and Savior Jesus Christ" (2 Peter 3:18).

Sounds exciting, doesn't it? Spiritual growth is God's will for your life. Yet, sadly, many Christians never mature. Once they're saved, they're satisfied. Imagine how grieved you would be as a parent if your baby never grew. That's how our heavenly Father feels when His children don't mature.

The chapters that follow in this book pinpoint areas in which I have counseled many Christians in their spiritual growth. God has honored this instruction in their lives, and I'm confident He'll use it to help you mature in Christ, too!

So let's get growing...

Two

Can I Be Sure of My Salvation?

These things I have written to you
who believe in the name of the Son of God,
in order that you may know
that you have eternal life.
1 John 5:13

The voice on the telephone trembled with stress. A woman was calling long distance to ask me to visit her mother who lived in my hometown. "She doesn't have long to live," the daughter informed me, "and she wants to make her peace with God."

I promised her I'd go right over. When I arrived, the husband ushered me into his wife's room. She was suffering from advanced cancer, and her physician had sent her home from the hospital to die. When I introduced myself as a pastor, she seemed relieved. Her first words were, "I know my time is short. Please tell me how I can go to heaven."

I shared the gospel message as simply as I could. The dear woman was glued to every word. Finally, I asked her if she had ever confessed her sins to God and placed her faith in Jesus as her personal Savior.

"Oh, yes," she answered without hesitation. "I did that many years ago."

"Was it a sincere commitment?" I asked. She assured me it was.

Assuming she might have misunderstood me, I reviewed the plan of salvation with her and then asked the same question from a different point of view. "Do you love Christ? And are you trusting in His death on the cross as your only hope of being right with God?"

"Absolutely," she replied.

After a bit more conversation with her, I came to the conclusion that her peace with God had been signed, sealed, and delivered long ago.

So I told her, "You're already a Christian! You're prepared to meet the Lord. If you should die today, you would go straight to heaven." A smile broke out on her face, but she could hardly believe it.

"Your only problem," I continued, "is that you don't have the assurance of your salvation." I then showed her from the Bible how she could be certain of her relationship with Christ.

That woman is one of many sincere believers I've counseled who have had peace with God but no peace in their hearts. They exemplify an important truth: Assurance isn't essential to our salvation, but it is essential to our peace of mind. Christians who aren't certain of their relationship with Christ aren't going to have fullness of joy. Nor are they prepared to serve the Lord.

Before we can rescue someone else from the quicksand of sin, we must have our own firm footing on the rock of assurance! Therefore, we shouldn't be satisfied until we know we're children of God on our way to heaven.

What Does the Bible Say?

Let's start with a promise of Christ in Revelation 3:20. "Behold, I stand at the door and knock [think of that as the door of your heart]; if anyone hears My voice and opens the door, I will come in to him, and will dine with him, and he with Me." Have you opened the door of your heart to the Lord Jesus? If so, He promised to come in. So He's living inside you now!

Next, read 1 John 5:11-12. "And the witness is this, that God has given us eternal life, and this life is in His Son. He who has the Son has the life; he who does not have the Son of God does not have the life." Here we learn that people who have Jesus living inside them possess eternal life. And people who don't have Christ don't possess eternal life. Nothing could be clearer than

All who trust in Christ can know they possess eternal life, whether they feel like it or not. It's not our feelings that settle the issue, but rather the facts of God's Word.

that black-and-white distinction drawn in this text of Scripture.

On that basis you can know for sure that you're on your way to heaven. The promise of God should be sufficient for each of His children. You don't have to lie awake at night singing the old hymn:

'Tis a point I long to know,
Oft it causes anxious thought—
Do I love the Lord, or no?
Am I His, or am I not?[1]

To buttress this truth further, the passage goes on to say in 1 John 5:13, "These things I have written to you who believe in the name of the Son of God, in order that you may know that you have eternal life."

Again, ask yourself, *Do I believe in the name of the Son of God?* If from your heart of hearts you can answer yes, then our heavenly Father wants you to know that you *have* (note the present tense) eternal life.

I think it's great that the Word of God does not say, "These things I have written to you who believe in the name of the Son of God, in order that you may *hope, think, wish, suppose,* or *dream* that you have eternal life." No! God made sure these things were written in His Word so that we might *know* eternal life is ours. In the same way that you know your name, address, and telephone number, our heavenly Father wants you to know that you're a Christian.

Look at another simple statement in the Bible. Jesus said in John 6:47, "Truly, truly, I say to you, he who believes has eternal life." There's nothing there about hoping, wishing, or thinking that we have eternal life. If we believe in Him, we have it! Our Lord's words couldn't be any clearer.

What about those times when you don't feel like a Christian? That doesn't change a thing! All who trust in Christ can know they possess eternal life, whether they feel like it or not. It's not our feelings that settle the issue, but rather the facts of God's Word.

Faith—The False and the True

Scripture makes it clear that faith in Christ is essential for salvation. That's where some people make a mistake. When they say they believe in Jesus, they mean, "I believe He lived on this earth and died on a cross" or "I believe in a God of creation."

If that's all a person believes, any assurance he might have of his salvation is sheer presumption. Not all faith is the genuine article. Suppose I ask a man, "Do you believe in communism?" If he answers yes, that could imply one of two things. He might mean that he believes communism exists, or he might mean that he is a Communist. What an enormous difference! You know communism exists, but that doesn't make you a Communist.

In like manner, faith in the truth that God exists or that Jesus lived and died doesn't make a person a Christian. Even demons believe (James 2:19). But that doesn't help them, because they neither love Him nor are dedicated to Him.

The usual phrase for "believing in" Christ is literally "believing *into*" Christ. For example, John 3:16 reads as follows in the original Greek language: "For God so loved the world, that He gave His only begotten Son, that whoever believes *into* Him should not perish, but have eternal life." To believe into Christ is to place your whole life into His. That involves love and commitment. Without that, our so-called faith is only a counterfeit.

Assurance must be based on substance. That substance is a faith in Christ that produces love for Him and dedication to Him.

"Can I be sure of my salvation?" you ask. You not only can, you must—if you want to grow!

What you must know to grow:

Assurance of eternal life isn't essential to your salvation, but it is essential to your peace, joy, effectiveness in Christian service, and spiritual growth. If you are trusting Christ as your personal Savior, and if this faith results in a sincere love for Him and commitment to Him, then our heavenly Father wants you to know that you're His child. If you should die today, you would go to heaven!

Simple-to-follow steps for Christian growth:

- Cease worrying about where you stand with Christ, and start making your life count for Him.
- Begin to grow from there!
- Memorize 1 John 5:11-13.

Note:
1. Anonymous hymn, "'Tis a Point I Long to Know" (no date).

Three

When Does God Get Even?

For God so loved the world,
that He gave His only begotten Son,
that whoever believes in Him should not perish,
but have eternal life.
John 3:16

I had just finished my sermon and given an invitation for people to invite Christ into their hearts. One young woman responded. Tears of joy were streaming down her cheeks. She had received her peace with God!

A few days later, I made a point to encourage her. She was grateful for our heavenly Father's pardon but still felt troubled by her past. She confessed to living with several men outside of marriage. One of them took his own life when she left him. She had become pregnant twice and aborted both babies. Now, she stared at me and said, "I know I'm forgiven, but I'm also afraid that one of these days God is going to get even."

Another new believer told me he had once murdered a man in cold blood. Still another admitted turning dozens of people on to drugs. Even Christians who have never indulged in notorious sins are often haunted by their past. Countless children of God are carrying a burdensome baggage of guilt in their hearts. Many of them share the fear of the young woman who said, "I'm afraid that one of these days God is going to get even."

Ever felt that way? That fear will surely stunt your growth. My purpose in this chapter is to help lift that burden off your heart. I want to show you how to have a clear conscience.

God Gets Even at the Cross!

I believe that Christians who fear punishment from God need to understand more clearly the death of Christ. Because our heavenly Father is just, He *must* punish sin. He can't look at us and say, "I love you so much that I'll just forget all about your sin. I'll ignore the whole thing and pretend it didn't happen." That would be mercy, but not justice. And when justice isn't satisfied, it leaves the guilty person with a feeling of uneasiness.

God's law was satisfied when Jesus died on the Cross. It would be unjust for God to exact a penalty twice for the same crime. And since Christ died for us, if our faith is in Him, it would be unfair of the Judge of the universe to punish us a second time.

God gets even with the Christian at the Cross. Romans 8:1 proves it: "There is therefore now no condemnation for those who are in Christ Jesus." That word *condemnation* could be translated "punishment." If you're in Christ, God won't punish you, because He already punished Jesus in your place.

Think of an old-fashioned shower with a bucket of water above it. A man gets into the shower and pulls the rope. The bucket turns over, spilling all its water on him. Now a second man steps into that same shower and pulls the rope. But he remains perfectly dry, because the water has already been poured out!

In that illustration, Jesus is the first man. God poured out His wrath on Christ in judgment for sin when He died on the Cross. Since by faith we stand in Jesus, there's no wrath left for us. So we don't have to fear that God will get even. He got even with us two thousand years ago at Calvary.

This doesn't mean our Lord won't discipline us. He will. Think of discipline as *correction.* That's far different from *punishment.* Discipline is given in love (Hebrews 12:6); punishment is the outbreak of wrath. Discipline proves we're forgiven children of God (Hebrews 12:7-8); punishment is reserved only for unrepentant rebels. God "disciplines us for *our* good, that we

How do we forgive ourselves? The same way God does—by looking to the Cross!

may share His holiness" (Hebrews 12:10). Punishment has no redeeming value.

God Forgives and Forgets

Rejoice in the following promises from the Bible concerning God's forgiveness:

- "As far as the east is from the west, so far has He removed our transgressions from us" (Psalm 103:12).
- "Thou hast cast all my sins behind Thy back" (Isaiah 38:17).
- "I, even I, am the one who wipes out your transgressions for My own sake; and I will not remember your sins" (Isaiah 43:25).
- "He will tread our iniquities underfoot. Yes, Thou wilt cast all their sins into the depths of the sea" (Micah 7:19).
- "Behold, the Lamb of God who takes away the sin of the world!" (John 1:29).
- "If we confess our sins, He is faithful and righteous to forgive us our sins and to cleanse us from all unrighteousness" (1 John 1:9).

A man and his wife were taking part in marriage counseling with their pastor. The wife complained, "Whenever Roy and I quarrel, he becomes historical."

The pastor interrupted to correct her. "You mean hysterical."

"No, historical! He's always digging up my past!"

Our sins aren't even history gathering dust in the archives of heaven. The archives don't exist anymore! Because God forgives *and* forgets, we have a clean slate.

I heard about another husband who asked his wife why she kept reminding him of a certain sin he had committed years earlier. "You promised to forgive and forget that," he complained.

"I *have* forgiven and forgotten," she answered. "But I don't want *you* to forget that I've forgiven and forgotten."

Unlike that wife, when our Lord buries the hatchet, He doesn't leave the handle sticking out for future use. He gets even, all right—at the Cross. Then He forgives and forgets!

Now Forgive Yourself

Al was a man I met in my hometown. I learned he was a Christian without a church home, so I invited him to ours. But he declined by saying, "It would be blasphemous for me to set foot in a house of God." Often, people who talk that way are only making an excuse in mock humility. But I sensed that Al's tone was different. So I asked him what he meant.

"I'm an alcoholic," he replied with deep shame. I asked a few more questions and learned that Al hadn't tasted alcohol in eight years. He had accepted God's forgiveness in Christ, but Al couldn't forgive himself. Consequently, he hadn't grown.

King David of Israel committed adultery with a woman named Bathsheba, then murdered her husband so he could marry her (2 Samuel 11). It was an outrageous crime against Uriah and the Lord. David wrestled with that for a long time. But when he accepted God's forgiveness, he also forgave himself. Twice in Psalm 32:1-2, in which he testified of the Lord's pardon, he called himself "blessed." The newer versions translate it "happy." David rediscovered his joy. And that can only mean he forgave himself.

The Apostle Paul claimed to be the worst sinner in history (1 Timothy 1:15). He had often persecuted disciples and voted for their executions (Acts 26:10). But as a forgiven man, he said he was "forgetting what *lies* behind" (Philippians 3:13). He also wrote, "I do not even judge myself" (1 Corinthians 4:3, *NIV*). God had pardoned his past, and Paul was able to leave it behind, too.

Have you forgiven yourself? To punish yourself with further guilt after coming to Christ is, in effect, to annul His suffering for you. It's like saying, "Father, I know the blood of Christ satisfies Your sense of justice. But it doesn't satisfy mine!" And thus we stand in judgment upon God when we refuse to forgive ourselves. More than that, we stifle our spiritual growth.

But just how do we forgive ourselves? The same way God does—by looking to the Cross! If you insist on getting even with yourself, go back to Calvary. Understand that your unwillingness to let yourself off the hook is another sin for which Christ died. So take it to the Cross and leave it there forever. And when you come back, you'll be ready to grow.

What you must know to grow:

God got even with you two thousand years ago, when His Son Jesus was punished in your place. He unleashed all His wrath on Him. Since your faith is in Christ, there is no condemnation—no punishment—waiting for you (Romans 8:1). Your conscience can and should be free from guilt.

Simple-to-follow steps for Christian growth:
● Accept God's pardoning love.
● Now forgive yourself. Do that the same way our heavenly Father forgives you—by looking to the Cross.
● Memorize John 3:16 and Romans 8:1.

Four

Why Am I Here?

You shall be My witnesses
both in Jerusalem, and in all Judea and Samaria,
and even to the remotest part of the earth.
Acts 1:8

Why am I here? What is my purpose in life supposed to be?

Have you ever asked yourself those questions? Many people couldn't begin to answer them. Without realizing it, their goal in life might be something like the pursuit of happiness or to make money or to love and be loved. But these and similar reasons for existence all fall short of the true mark.

The Christian's purpose in life is quite specific. In this chapter, I want to share that purpose with you, because if you don't know what it is, you'll waste a lot of time spinning your wheels. I like the way some believers who call themselves The Navigators put it:

Our purpose in life is to know Christ and to make Him known.

To Know Christ

The famous evangelist Billy Graham once said that Donald Barnhouse knew Scripture better than anyone he had ever met.[1] Barnhouse was practically a walking Bible encyclopedia!

He had a "lifetime verse" that dominated everything he did. It might surprise you to hear it. It came from Philippians 3:10, which begins, "that I may know Him [Christ]." Donald Barnhouse's great pursuit in life was to know the Lord Jesus more and more. He could never get enough of Him.

And neither can we!

"What were we made for?" asks J. I. Packer. "To know God. What aim should we set ourselves in life? To know God. What is the 'eternal life' that Jesus gives? Knowledge of God (John 17:3). What is the best thing in life, bringing more joy, delight, and contentment than anything else? Knowledge of God.... Once you become aware that the main business that you are here for is to know God, most of life's problems fall into place of their own accord."[2]

You might be thinking, *Since I'm a Christian, I already know Christ.*

True. But you've only just begun your personal relationship with Him. When Paul wrote Philippians 3:10 and testified that his goal was to know Christ, he had been a believer for nearly thirty years. Because Jesus is the infinite God, we human beings can never know Him fully.

Do you know America? In a sense you do. Perhaps you've lived in it all your life. You might be able to name the fifty states and all their capitals. You may have even visited every state and its capital. But you could still spend the rest of your life exploring America's lakes, canyons, forests, caves, farmlands, rivers, and mountains. The United States has more than 250 million people, most of whom you've never met. In a very real sense, you *don't* know America.

And so with our relationship to Christ. No matter how long we've known Him, there's always more to discover. Sadly, many people have been Christians for decades and have scarcely begun to get acquainted with the Lord. The average church has more than its share of members who live in shocking ignorance of Jesus Christ.

But God has revealed Himself in the Bible, and that means He wants to be known. While you and I can't know the Lord *completely*, we can know Him *well*. This

The gospel is not just something to go to church to hear, but to go from church to tell!

is what the Christian life is all about—walking with Jesus day by day so that we understand Him more and more. This will increase our love for the Lord. Truly, *to know Him is to love Him!*

To Make Him Known

As you grow in your knowledge of Christ, you'll want others to know Him, too. Nothing will bring you greater joy than the privilege of introducing someone to the Lord Jesus. This is one of the best ways to grow spiritually. But tragically, many are not sharing their faith. They've known Christ for years, but they've never led anyone else to Him. They're consistent in church attendance and Bible reading, but they're not making Christ known.

That kind of believer is like a person who spends a lot of time eating but none exercising. He or she is going to be overweight and out of shape! If you want to grow spiritually, it's vital that you do both. You should be well-fed through reading Scripture, hearing it taught by others, getting involved in small-group Bible study, and reading good Christian books. That's your spiritual intake. But you must balance that with proper spiritual exercise. That occurs when you share your faith, knowledge, and love for Christ with other people. The gospel is not just something to go *to* church to hear, but to go *from* church to tell!

The last words someone speaks in life are always cherished by those who loved him or her. The final words of Christ, before He ascended back into heaven, are recorded for us in Acts 1:8: "But you shall receive power when the Holy Spirit has come upon you; and you shall be My witnesses both in Jerusalem, and in all Judea and Samaria, and even to the remotest part of the earth." That's why we're here—to spread the fragrance of Christ throughout the world.

Underscore the word *witnesses* in Acts 1:8. Someone has said, "God hasn't equipped many of us to be lawyers, but He has subpoenaed all of us as witnesses." A witness is someone who testifies to a firsthand experience. Since we know Christ personally, we can witness to His love, forgiveness, grace, and life-changing power. After all, He has loved us, forgiven our sins, shown us grace, and changed our lives.

Witnessing means sharing a verbal testimony with other people—telling them what Jesus has done for us and what He can do for them. It also includes a living testimony. Dishonesty in business, profane speech, and a worldly life-style give off a witness, too. They tell others that Jesus hasn't really changed us. And that reflects poorly on Him. So we must be careful to undergird our verbal testimony with a living testimony.

Tomorrow morning when you get out of bed, there will be approximately 138,000 more lost people in the world than there were this morning. That figure grows by about one million per week and 52 million per year. A line composed of all the people who don't know Christ would circle the earth thirty times. And this line extends at the rate of twenty miles a day.[3]

A staggering thought? Too staggering for some. They hear statistics like that and say, "What's the use of trying to win people to the Lord? We'll never reach them all."

I'm reminded of a man who saw thousands of starfish washed up on the beach. He began picking them up and throwing them into the ocean, one at a time. Another man came along and said, "That's a hopeless task! You'll never get all those starfish back in the water! What good can you possibly be doing?"

The first man showed him the starfish in his hand, and after flinging it into the ocean, replied, "To that one starfish, I just did a lot of good!"

How do you win the world for Christ? One person at a time!

Most Christians know they *should* share their faith, but they don't know *how*. For practical help, I recommend an evangelism training course. Often, these are taught in churches. Perhaps the most popular one is Evangelism Explosion. Ask your pastor about it or another seminar that will give you practical, hands-on training in sharing your faith.

Here are some excellent books that also teach simple, practical ways to make Christ known:

Aldrich, Joe. *Gentle Persuasion: Creative Ways to Introduce Your Friends to Christ*. Portland, OR: Multnomah Press, 1988.

Aldrich, Joe. *Life-Style Evangelism*. Portland, OR: Multnomah Press, 1981.

Bright, Bill. *Witnessing Without Fear: How to Share Your Faith with Confidence*. San Bernardino, CA: Here's Life Publishers, 1987.

Kennedy, D. James. *Evangelism Explosion*. Wheaton, IL: Tyndale House Publishers, 1970.

Little, Paul. *How to Give Away Your Faith*. Downer's Grove, IL: InterVarsity Press, 1962.

Pippert, Rebecca. *Out of the Saltshaker and Into the World*. Downer's Grove, IL: InterVarsity Press, 1979.

What you must know to grow:

God's purpose for you on earth is to know Christ and to make Him known.

Simple-to-follow steps for Christian growth:

• Get to know Jesus personally through His Word, the

Bible. This is the most fulfilling relationship you'll ever experience.

● With the Holy Spirit's help, seek to introduce others to Christ so that they might know Him personally, too.

● For practical instruction in sharing your faith, enroll in an evangelism training class. These are usually offered in local churches.

● Read one or more of the books recommended at the end of this chapter.

● Memorize Acts 1:8.

Notes:

1. This indirect quotation comes from *Eternity* magazine shortly after the death of Donald Barnhouse in 1960.

2. J. I. Packer, *Knowing God* (Downer's Grove, IL: InterVarsity Press, 1973), p. 29.

3. The information in this paragraph is derived from articles appearing in the following publications: *The Heaven and Home Hour* news bulletin, January, 1985; *Peninsula Covenant Church Bridge*, December, 1983.

Five

What Do You Mean, Fifteen Minutes a Day Will Change My Life?

All Scripture is inspired by God and profitable
for teaching, for reproof, for correction,
for training in righteousness; that the man of God
may be adequate, equipped for every good work.
2 Timothy 3:16-17

The source of lasting change in a person's life is not wealth, success in the business world, or a happy marriage. Rather, it is in a relationship with Christ that is rooted in and sustained by the Scriptures. So dramatic is the change at Christian conversion that the Apostle Paul says we become "new creatures" (2 Corinthians 5:17, *KJV*).

But change does not stop at conversion. It continues as the believer grows in his or her knowledge of the Bible. For that reason it is good to discipline yourself to read the Bible daily. And if you invest just fifteen minutes a day in the Word, you will never be the same!

When people come to me for pastoral counseling, I ask them if they're getting alone with God each day in His Word. The vast majority of them answer no. I always promise that if they carve out just fifteen minutes in their daily schedules for the study of Scripture, God will change their lives.

And He does!

Don't get me wrong. I'm not promoting the Bible as a lucky charm. It doesn't exempt us from difficulties. It's not as if a chapter a day keeps the devil away. But when a Christian is regularly listening to the voice of his Lord, he gains wisdom to deal with his problems and strength to be joyful in the midst of them.

Only One Percent of Your Day

Fifteen minutes is about one percent of your day. Will you set aside that much time to listen to God? You'll never regret it. How do I know? Because I made this commitment years ago, and it was the turning point in my Christian life.

I was eighteen years old and a freshman in college. God was speaking to my heart about my lack of spiritual power and ignorance of Scripture. So I made a personal vow. I wasn't going to let anything come between me and God's truth. I wouldn't allow myself to go to bed at night until I had spent at least a quarter of an hour reading my Bible.

My time was filled with classes, studies, practicing with the tennis team, and a part-time job. I was busy—just like you are now. The first day I had studied till past midnight and was exhausted. Just when I was ready to collapse into bed, I remembered that I hadn't yet made time for my devotions. So I lived up to my promise. I forced myself to listen to God's voice in the pages of Scripture for fifteen minutes before calling it a night.

The next few days were similar, and I was tired of paying the penalty for procrastination. So I made time in the morning to meet with the Lord. Soon, this became a habit. My life began to take on new meaning. I was excited about living for Christ and growing in His grace. I had cultivated an appetite for Scripture, and God was satisfying me.

Since then, I've read the Bible through dozens of times. And these many years of practice have taught me that it's best to have your quiet time in the Word at the beginning of the day. Putting it off until bedtime is like tuning your instrument after the concert or loading your gun after the battle.

A friend of mine lives by the slogan, "No Bible, no breakfast." He won't let himself taste food until he's fed himself on the Word of God. Of course, any time of day you read Scripture is better than none. But for most people the best time is early in the morning. It will prepare you for what lies ahead and start your day in a spiritual frame of mind and heart.

But I must warn you: You'll never find this time. You'll have to make time. I once noticed a sign on my secretary's desk that read, "You always have time for what you put first." I thought, *That's the secret to getting into the Bible on a daily basis.* Settle it now that God's Word is going to be your number-one priority every day. Make this commitment between you and God. Then stick to it.

Cover to Cover in Less Than a Year

I learned that at the rate of fifteen minutes a day, I could read the entire Bible in less than a year. And I'm not even a fast reader! Just think. By starting today, at a mere rate of a quarter of an hour per day, twelve months from now you will have covered all sixty-six books of the Bible!

If you doubt that, then try this test. Divide the number of pages in your Bible by 365. The result is the number of pages you'll need to cover each day to read your Bible through in a year. This will be about four pages or less. Now see how long it takes you to read those four pages. If you can do it in a quarter of an hour, you've proven that you can read the Bible from cover to cover in a year at the rate of fifteen minutes a day!

Start at the beginning of the New Testament, not the Old. Read the first four pages in the Gospel of Matthew. Stop where the biblical chapter ends on page 4. Place a bookmark there. The following day you'll know right where you left off. Just open to the page with the bookmark and read four more pages. Follow that pattern each day, and you'll take in all of God's Word in a year. Five years from now you will have read through Scripture five times. In ten years you'll be a Bible whiz!

"Ten years?" you might ask. "That's a long time!"

Granted. But where will you be in ten years if you don't start reading the Bible? You'll be right where you are now—probably not even there, because life isn't static. If we don't grow, we decline. And no one wants to do that.

Right now you might be thinking, *But I can never remember what I've read in the Bible!* Ernie Nickell, a farmer in his 70's when I led him to Christ, said that to me.

I told him the story of a man who wanted to fill a tank with water. He turned on a faucet, filled up his bucket, and carried it over to the tank. He made many trips back and forth. But there was one problem—his bucket had holes in it. By the time he walked over to the tank, all the water had leaked out.

Ernie looked at me, as if to say, "Yeah, that's what happens to me when I read the Bible."

So I replied, "This man's work wasn't a total waste. At least he had a clean bucket. So even if some facts leak out of your memory while reading Scripture, at least you're going to have your mind, heart, and life continually cleansed!"

That was several years ago. In each year since then Ernie has read the Bible from cover to cover. And every year he reports to me, "Guess what? My 'bucket' has fewer holes in it."

He's growing. And so will you.

Which Version of the Bible Is Best for You?

As a new Christian you need to read a simple version of Scripture. This is not the time to worry about which translation is the most precise. I've enjoyed reading through all of them, as well as the original Greek New Testament, and I'd say that every version of the Bible is worth reading.

For a brand-new believer, I recommend *The Living Bible*. You don't have to limit yourself to this one ver-

A systematic, daily reading of Scripture is the most important discipline to establish for growth in the Christian life.

sion, however. But it will give you a clear understanding of God's Word, because it paraphrases the text—it doesn't substitute exact English words for the original Hebrew and Greek ones. For now, it is not necessary to concern yourself with the more technical translations of Scripture. You need to get the big picture. And nothing can give it to you better than *The Living Bible*. Personally, I've found it more spiritually refreshing than any other version of God's Word.

A systematic, daily reading of Scripture is the most important discipline to establish for growth in the Christian life. In doing so, you will experience increase of your faith, and you will understand God's plan for your life. There is no substitute for daily feeding on the Word of God.

But let me add a note of caution. Reading from Genesis through Revelation isn't an end in itself. The goal is to hear God speak personally to you so that He can change you. Therefore, when *you* go through the Bible, make sure *the Bible* goes through you! Mastering Scripture isn't nearly as important as allowing Scripture to master you. The Word of the Lord was written that we might know the Lord of the Word.

What you must know to grow:

You must know God's Word as it speaks personally to you. A daily discipline of Bible reading will put you in touch with the living Christ and change your life. This will make the difference in your experience between spiritual victory or defeat, fulfillment or frustration, joy or weariness.

Simple-to-follow steps for Christian growth:

- Set aside at least fifteen minutes each day to listen to God's voice in the pages of Scripture.
- Proceed straight through the Bible, beginning with the New Testament in the Gospel of Matthew.
- Claim God's promises.
- Obey God's revealed will.
- Take seriously His warnings against sin.
- Find your wisdom for living in God's Word.
- Learn from it how to trust the Lord for every problem, trial, and worry.
- Memorize 2 Timothy 3:16-17.

Six

I Tried to Live for Christ, But It Didn't Work

The *life* which I now live in the flesh
I live by faith in the Son of God,
who loved me and delivered Himself up for me.
Galatians 2:20

Some time ago, I was visiting in the home of a new couple in our community. When I introduced myself as a pastor, both husband and wife freely talked of spiritual things. I asked them if they had ever invited Jesus Christ into their hearts as personal Savior.

An embarrassed look came over their faces as they each admitted doing that several years earlier. "But nothing ever came of it," they explained. "We tried to live for Christ, but it didn't work."

I've heard that same basic confession more times than I care to remember. And whenever someone utters it, I know he or she is living in spiritual defeat.

The greatest frustration in the Christian life occurs when you try to live for Jesus Christ. It can't be done. No matter how moral you become, you'll never be able to please God in your own strength.

There is only one person who can live as a Christian should—Jesus. The secret, then, to honoring God with your life is to let Christ, who already lives *in* you, live *through* you!

Finally, I'm in Business!

Ian Thomas, a noted British Bible teacher, had served for seven years as a young pastor desperately trying to do something for God. One night he knelt at his bedside, wept, and prayed, "Lord, I'm tired, burned out, defeated, and I quit!"

He testified that he felt as if God sighed up in heaven, then replied, "Finally, I'm in business! I've been waiting for this moment for seven years! Ian, you've been so busy living *for* Me that you haven't allowed Me to live *through* you."

It was a new concept to Ian Thomas. He decided that from then on he'd merely be an empty vessel through which the dynamic power of Jesus Christ could flow. After that experience, his ministry began to touch people all over the world through his teaching ministry at Capernwray Bible Institute in England and through his many books.

Have you been trying your best to live for the Lord? Forget it. Only Jesus Christ can please the heavenly Father. The fulfilling Christian life isn't a matter of brute determination. You can clench your fists, set your jaw, and promise until doomsday that you're going to glorify God, but it'll never happen as long as you attempt it in your own strength.

A little boy once asked Donald Barnhouse to sign his autograph in his Bible. The famous Bible teacher wrote:

It is not what you do for Christ that counts;
it is what you let Him do through you![1]

It's a simple lesson and yet one many Christians have a hard time learning.

Hudson Taylor, one of the greatest missionaries in church history, said near the end of his life, "I used to ask God to help me. Then I asked if I might help Him. I ended up by asking Him to do His work through me."[2] That's why Hudson Taylor had such abundant fruitfulness on the mission field.

In Philippians 4:13 the Apostle Paul wrote, "I can do all things *through Him who strengthens me.*" Hebrews 13:20-21 clearly states that it is "*the God of peace*" who is "working in us that which is pleasing in His sight." And Ephesians 3:20 teaches that God "is able to do exceeding abundantly beyond all that we ask or think, *according to the power that works within us.*"

Our job is to quit trying to live for Jesus and simply become empty channels through which He can live His own life.

A verse in a familiar hymn by George Duffield, Jr. expresses this essential truth:

> Stand up, stand up for Jesus,
> Stand in His strength alone;
> The arm of flesh will fail you—
> Ye dare not trust your own![3]

Three Simple Lessons

I heard about a believer who stood up in a testimonial meeting in his church and said, "I spent forty-two years learning three simple lessons. First, that nothing I could do in my own strength would please God. Second, that God didn't expect me to please Him in my own strength. And third, that God had already provided the power, through the indwelling Christ, by which I could please Him!"

I don't want you to waste forty-two years learning those lessons. Our job is to quit trying to live for Jesus and simply become empty channels through which He can live His own life. God can't have His way while we're in the way. Only when we get out of the way can the Lord use us.

That's what Mary E. Maxwell had in mind when she wrote in her hymn:

> Channels only, blessed Master,
> But with all Thy wondrous pow'r
> Flowing through us, Thou canst use us,
> Every day and ev'ry hour![4]

What a liberating truth to realize that God isn't looking for some stellar performance on our part by which we try to imitate His Son! No, our heavenly Father only asks that we yield ourselves to the power of the indwelling Christ, that He might manifest His own life through us.

This is what the Apostle Paul was getting at when he shared this testimony: "I have been crucified with Christ; and it is no longer I who live, but Christ lives in me" (Galatians 2:20).

Imagine a man who strains to push his car when all along it has a powerful engine inside. He doesn't know about the motor, so he thinks it's his job to get the car rolling. He needs to come to the point where he says, "It is no longer I who push the car, but the motor that does the work!"

We Christians are sometimes like that man. We assume that the power for Christian service must come from within ourselves. We need to learn to say along with Paul, "It is no longer I who live, but Christ lives in me." Until we make that discovery, we're going to be totally frustrated.

What About Christian Discipline?

At this point a word of clarification is in order. There are commands in the Bible that tell us to "strive, wrestle, train, mortify, contend, make every effort," and "be disciplined." Do they contradict what I'm saying in this chapter? Not at all. It takes that kind of steadfastness to remain yielded to Christ. We should be laboring for our Lord—but in His strength, not our own.

Suppose you have a serious illness. Your physician prescribes some pills for you and says, "Be sure to take these every four hours. If you do, you'll get well." You don't want to remain ill, so you discipline yourself to follow his orders. You live on a schedule of taking the pills every fours hours around the clock. You even get up at midnight and four in the morning. And sure enough, you get well.

Now then, what was the power that brought about your healing? Was it your personal discipline? No, it was the medicine! And so it is in our Christian lives. God commands us to be disciplined. But it's not our practice of discipline that brings spiritual growth. It's the power of the indwelling Christ.

The Transference of Power

To unleash Christ's power in your life, make this commitment in prayer: "Lord Jesus, I surrender the control of my body over to You. I want You to look through my eyes. From now on You will think through my mind. My ears will now be Your ears. Use my tongue as Your mouthpiece. Here are my hands. Reach out to other people by means of them. From now on, my feet will only move at Your direction, because they're going to be Your feet. And I ask You to love through my heart. It's no longer the strength of my feelings and emotions, but Yours."

That kind of surrender isn't easy. Our old nature doesn't like to give its life away, even to Jesus Christ. That's why He said that His followers must take up their crosses daily (Luke 9:23). Each morning as we take up our cross, our bodies become instruments of Christ. We are crucified people, nevertheless we live in Christ. Resurrection power takes over and that's when the living Christ performs His own work through us.

It all sounds so simple, doesn't it? Too simple for some. Perhaps that's why so many believers have missed it. Their intentions are great—to live for the glory of God. But their power is insufficient. As Jesus said, "The spirit is willing, but the flesh is weak" (Matthew 26:41).

The greatest frustration in the Christian life is something that need never trouble you. All the power you'll ever require to glorify God is available to you. But it's not something you create, just something you release. When you learn that secret, your spiritual life ceases to be frustrating and starts to be fulfilling.

What you must know to grow:

Your best efforts to live for Christ in your own strength will result in constant failure and frustration. Only Jesus can please the heavenly Father.

Simple-to-follow steps for Christian growth:

- Surrender yourself to the indwelling Christ.
- Make a conscious commitment each day to be a channel through which the Lord Jesus can bear His own fruit of holiness and love.
- Memorize Galatians 2:20.

Notes:
1. Margaret N. Barnhouse, *That Man Barnhouse* (Wheaton, IL: Tyndale House Publishers, 1986), p. 30.
2. Quoted in *Pulpit Helps* (Chattanooga, TN: AMG International, Nov. 1983), p. 20.
3. From George Duffield's hymn, "Stand Up, Stand Up for Jesus," 1858. Public domain.
4. From Mary E. Maxwell's hymn, "Channels Only," 1910. Public domain.

Seven

Why Do I Feel Like a Walking Civil War?

Or do you not know
that your body is a temple
of the Holy Spirit who is in you,
whom you have from God,
and that you are not your own?
1 Corinthians 6:19

Carlos was a new Christian who met with me on Saturday mornings for discipleship training. He was joyful in Christ and growing rapidly. One morning he arrived in a sense of awe and told me, "I've made a great discovery! I read this week in the Bible that I'm involved in a spiritual warfare. I thought the Christian life was more like a walk in the park than a battle—but I was wrong!"

I smiled and said, "You're learning, Carlos! You're learning."

My purpose in this chapter is to help you understand that you now have two natures. Even though God has given you new life in Christ, the old sinful nature does not want to surrender. It will constantly try to divert you from fellowship with the Lord.

Two Opposing Forces

Perhaps the clearest verse on this is Galatians 5:17 in *The Living Bible*: "For we naturally love to do evil things that are just the opposite from the things that the Holy Spirit tells us to do; and the good things we want to do when the Spirit has His way with us are just the opposite of our natural desires. These two forces within us are constantly fighting each other to win control over us, and our wishes are never free from their pressures."

The Christian is a walking civil war. Every time your old nature wants to sin, your new nature says, "You must not do that!" And each time the divine nature God implanted in you decides to honor Christ, the sinful nature tries to dissuade you. The battle never ceases between these two superpowers.

Suppose another person hurts your feelings. Something inside you says, "You should never forgive him for what he did!" That's the old nature talking. At this point your Christian nature interrupts: "I'm not going to let you feel comfortable with that attitude! God could have taken revenge against you for all your sins against Him, but He pardoned you instead. Now it's your turn to forgive." And thus the Christian is pulled in two directions—sinfulness and holiness.

Which Dog Are You Feeding?

A missionary was trying to explain this conflict to one of his new converts. "It's like two dogs fighting inside your heart," he said, "a good dog and a bad dog."

Hearing that, the new believer asked a very practical question: "Which dog wins?"

The missionary thought for a moment, then answered, "The one you feed the most!"

Which nature are you feeding the most? The one that hungers after sin or the new nature Christ gives you with its desire for holiness? Believers who watch unwholesome movies and television programs, read lustful books and magazines, and seek to be "in" with people who despise Christ are feeding the old nature. It's no wonder their spiritual lives are in shambles! To feed the new nature, we must invest time in the Word of God, prayer, worship, and Christian fellowship.

Which of those two alternatives sounds more attractive to you? The answer reveals which nature you've recently been feeding.

A woman once shared with me an experience that changed her life. She had made herself some goodies in the kitchen and stacked them high on her plate. Then she reclined in her easy chair and got ready to enjoy her

The next time some evil tendency tugs at your heart, don't push the panic button. Learn now that your old nature will be at war with you until the moment you step into heaven.

ı

favorite television program. There's nothing wrong with that. But for many days she had been neglecting the Lord in prayer, Bible study, and the church. She was a Christian, but her life was out of balance.

In her mind she started hearing these words: "Feed the flesh! Feed the flesh!" They became louder: "FEED THE FLESH! FEED THE FLESH!" The words began to thunder in her spiritual ears.

Now this woman isn't the kind who hears audible voices from God, but this message was a distinct impression, and she took it to heart. She couldn't enjoy her program that night. She had to retreat to her bedroom, where she knelt and recommitted herself in a practical way to Jesus Christ.

The Holy Spirit within her had declared war on her old nature, and that night He won.

Once I was counseling a young woman who was having an affair with a married man. When I shared the good news of Christ's love and forgiveness, she repented of her sins and received Him by faith. Later, the man divorced his wife and begged the new Christian to marry him. She told me, "I still have feelings for him, so maybe it *is* God's will for me to be his wife."

That remark told me she didn't understand the warfare between the two natures inside her. She thought that if her feelings told her to do something, it was a sign of God's leading. But her feelings were waging war against her faith.

I must be honest and point out that some Christians don't believe the old nature lives on in the new believer. They claim that once you accept Christ, the sinful self is gone forever. They quote Romans 6:6, which teaches that "our old self was crucified with *Him* [Christ]." But the end of that verse makes it clear that the old nature is dead to sin's *domination*. It concludes with these words: "...that we should no longer be slaves to sin."

The sinful nature is no longer our master, but it's still our enemy! And so the civil war continues.

I doubt that anyone in church history has experienced a closer walk with Christ than Charles Spurgeon, the great nineteenth-century London preacher. But even he confessed, "I have a daily fighting of my better self against the old self, the newborn nature against the old nature, which will, if it can, still keep its hold upon me."[1] Yes, even the holiest of Christians feels the inner conflict. So don't be discouraged when the battle rages inside you.

We might compare a Christian to a water faucet that continually drips cold water. No matter how hard you turn that right nozzle to the "off" position, you can't stop the flow of the cold water. But by turning the left nozzle to the "on" position, you can send out a stream of hot water that dominates the cold. That hot water is like the power of our Christian nature. If we give it full play, it can win the victory over the unending trickle of sin and self.

Don't Be Caught Off Guard

Why do I bring all this up? Because I'm trying to save you from despair. Christians who don't realize they still possess a wicked nature encounter serious doubts of their salvation when they feel drawn toward sin. The next time some evil tendency tugs at your heart, don't push the panic button. Learn now that your old nature will be at war with you until the moment you step into heaven.

The important thing is to stay in the battle. Don't give up, and don't give in. Keep starving the old nature and feeding the new. You'll never reach perfection in this life. But if your new nature rules over the old, the world will see a dynamic difference in you. And that will bring glory to God!

What you must know to grow:

As a Christian you have two natures inside you—the old, sinful self and the new, divine nature. These will always be at war. The old nature will tug you toward sin, and the new nature will draw you toward holiness. Don't be discouraged by this spiritual warfare.

Simple-to-follow steps for Christian growth:

- Feed the new nature and starve the old!
- Be disciplined in prayer.
- Soak your mind and heart in God's Word.
- Memorize key verses of Scripture.
- Join a small-group Bible study.
- Cultivate fellowship and friendships with other Christians; avoid places, people, and things that will interfere with your spiritual walk.
- Memorize 1 Corinthians 6:19-20.

Note:
1. Charles H. Spurgeon (Tom Carter, editor), *Spurgeon At His Best* (Grand Rapids, MI: Baker Book House, 1988), p. 132.

Eight

Aren't All Christians the Same?

But the fruit of the Spirit
is love, joy, peace, patience,
kindness, goodness, faithfulness,
gentleness, self-control;
against such things there is no law.
Galatians 5:22-23

I was an 18-year-old college freshman, flying home from Seattle to San Francisco for the Christmas holidays; I had never been on a commercial airliner before. The flight attendant asked me if I wanted to have lunch. I was starving at the time, but I politely declined the meal. And I wasn't even airsick. I turned the lunch down because I thought I would have to pay for it. I didn't understand that it was already included in the price of the ticket.

Of course, I reached San Francisco, just like everyone else on the plane. But they had a more enjoyable flight than I. They arrived with satisfied stomachs, while I was hungry. And when I learned that I had turned down a free meal, I was also angry—with myself.

As I look back on that experience, I see in it a picture of two types of Christians. All believers are going to heaven. But some enjoy the trip, while others make it a rough ride.

Aren't all Christians the same? you ask. No! The second and third chapters of 1 Corinthians teach that there are two kinds of believers, the carnal and the spiritual.

The Carnal Christian

The carnal believer is a person who belongs to Christ but doesn't live like it. He is supposed to be under the control of the Holy Spirit, but, instead, he's dominated by his sinful nature. In 1 Corinthians 3:1, the Apostle Paul writes, "And I, brethren, could not speak to you as to spiritual men, but as to men of flesh [translated "carnal" in another version], as to babes in Christ." Notice, Paul calls them "brethren" and says they are "in Christ," yet they are "men of flesh" or carnal.

At this point I must warn you that a few Bible teachers claim there is no such thing as a carnal Christian. They say that if you're not sold out to Jesus Christ, you're not a child of God. I believe they're overreacting. A man who doesn't take showers is not a pig; he's a man who doesn't take showers! Likewise, a Christian who doesn't live like one isn't a non-Christian; he's a carnal believer. Someone once said that he has just enough Christianity to be miserable in a bar, but not enough to be happy in a prayer meeting.

The first thing we learn about a carnal Christian is that *he is not growing.* In 1 Corinthians 3:2-3 Paul goes on to say, "I gave you milk to drink, not solid food; for you were not yet able *to receive it.* Indeed, even now you are not yet able, for you are still fleshly [carnal]." It's natural to be a milk-fed baby at birth. But to remain an infant for years is a tragedy. And sadly, the carnal Christian doesn't mature spiritually because he has no desire to grow.

Second, *a carnal Christian is a disappointment to Christ.* Paul goes on to rebuke the Corinthians with these words: "Even now . . . you are still fleshly [carnal]. . . . are you not walking like mere men?" (vv. 2-3). The Apostle is saying something like this: "After all this time that you've been Christians, and with all the teaching you've heard, is a carnal life the only thing you have to show for yourselves? You've had plenty of time to mature into spiritual men and women, but you still live like non-believers!"

Every church has people just like that. They disappoint the Lord, the pastor, and themselves. The only one they please is Satan. They can't be relied on for service;

*As we humble ourselves,
God's Spirit fills more
and more of us, thereby
gaining control over our
minds, emotions, and
wills.*

they reduce the church's strength when they should be adding to it; they're supposed to be out witnessing and living for Christ. But, instead, the church leaders have to babysit them.

Third, *a carnal Christian is not a victorious believer.* This is obvious from Paul's words in the middle of verse 3: "For since there is jealousy and strife among you, are you not fleshly [carnal]?" We're supposed to be known for our love and unity. So when there is "jealousy and strife" in our camp, it's a sure sign of defeat for our cause.

Jealousy and strife are two examples of the sins that victimize a carnal believer. Others are these: He has little or no prayer life; he's not reading his Bible; and instead of trusting the Lord to solve his problems, he worries about them.

One day I saw a Christian friend of mine lose his temper at someone who provoked him. Later my friend was feeling guilty about that and apologized to me, but not without offering an excuse: "After what that man did to me, it was only natural for me to get angry at him!"

He couldn't have been more correct. It *was* only natural. But, Christians are supposed to be *supernatural* people! Of course we all make mistakes and commit sins; nobody's perfect. But that doesn't give us an excuse for living carnally.

The Spiritual Christian

In contrast to the carnal believer, the spiritual one is fully surrendered to the power of the Holy Spirit. He doesn't play at being a Christian. At the end of 1 Corinthians 2, Paul first talks about the spiritual Christian's *perception.* He "appraises all things" (v. 15). That means he sees life from God's point of view.

As a result, when trials come his way, he understands that the Lord is shaping him into the image of Christ. When tragedies strike, the spiritual believer doesn't become bitter against his Master. Instead, he encourages himself in the knowledge that God works all things together for his good (Romans 8:28).

Second, Paul goes on to talk about the spiritual Christian's *possession*. He has "the mind of Christ" (1 Corinthians 2:16). That means he regards sin as Jesus did—as a deadly enemy that is good only for crucifixion. Because he has the mind of Christ, he knows better than to love worldliness. "The mind of Christ" leads the spiritual believer to humble himself in an attitude of servanthood to others. "The mind of Christ" is also sensitive to people who are spiritually lost.

The Difference—The Filling of the Holy Spirit

The difference between a carnal and a spiritual Christian hinges on what Ephesians 5:18 calls the filling of the Holy Spirit. Put simply, a believer is filled with God's Spirit when he or she is under His control. It's not as if we need more of the Holy Spirit, because we received all there is of Him when we trusted Christ as Savior. But often He doesn't possess all there is of us.

Suppose you have four ounces of milk in the refrigerator, and you pour it into an eight-ounce glass. The glass has all of the milk, but the milk doesn't fill the glass. Half of the glass remains untouched by the milk. That's a picture of us and the Holy Spirit. Like that glass, we need to shrink in size to be filled. As we humble ourselves, God's Spirit fills more and more of us, thereby gaining control over our minds, emotions, and wills. And when God exercises authority over every part of us, we are filled with the Spirit!

Or think of a glove and a hand. The glove is lifeless by itself. But when the hand fills it, the glove can do great things! Now what if the glove is filled with paper? There's no room for the hand. And, as a result, the glove can't fulfill its purpose.

You are the glove, and the Holy Spirit is the hand. God created you to be filled with His Spirit. That means you must be emptied of self and yielded to the Spirit's control. When you are, you'll be a Christian who makes a difference that will last throughout eternity!

What you must know to grow:

All Christians are not the same! There are two kinds— the carnal and the spiritual. Both belong to Christ. But there is an enormous difference in their life-styles. The carnal Christian is under the control of his old, sinful nature, while the spiritual Christian lives under the control of the Holy Spirit.

Simple-to-follow steps for Christian growth:

- Submit to the indwelling Spirit's control in your life.
- Allow Him to dominate your personality.
- Consciously yield yourself every day to His holy influence.
- Memorize Galatians 5:22-23.

Nine

What's the Difference Between Temptation and Sin?

God is faithful, who will not allow you to be tempted
beyond what you are able, but with the temptation
will provide the way of escape also,
that you may be able to endure it.
1 Corinthians 10:13

Temptation and sin are two cousins who often mas querade as identical twins. I used to assume th every believer understood the difference between then But I've learned to ask new disciples, "What's the diffe ence between temptation and sin?" Seldom do the answer my question correctly.

I've witnessed many spiritual casualties on the road Christian growth that stem from ignorance in this are: So in this chapter I'm going to share with you the fou vital distinctions between temptation and sin.

Temptation Is a Suggestion; Sin Is a Yielding to the Suggestion

Probably the biggest fallacy Christians have on th issue is that temptation takes place in our minds, an sin occurs in our actions. That's not always true. It possible to sin in our thought lives without lifting finger. The real difference is that temptation is a sugges tion, and sin is a yielding to the suggestion, all of whicl can take place right in our minds.

Picture yourself waiting in your car in front of a re light at a busy intersection. Suddenly you spot a ma walking across the street who recently humiliated you i public. Instantly this thought flashes through you mind: *Why don't you just step on the gas and run him over?* That's the temptation! It's only a suggestion— maybe a strong one—but still, only a suggestion.

Of course you don't want to become a murderer, so you resist the urge to kill him. You may even smile and noc at him as he walks by. But in your heart and mind you are running him over, and you're enjoying every bit of your fantasy.

Now that's sin! You haven't lifted a finger outwardly, but you've done plenty inwardly. Although only your thought life has been affected, that's enough to make you guilty of sin in God's eyes.

This is why Jesus could say, "Everyone who is angry with his brother shall be guilty" of murder, and "Everyone who looks on a woman to lust for her has committed adultery with her already in his heart" (Matthew 5:22,28). God doesn't look just on the outward act; He judges the heart.

To avoid sinning in that situation, you could have denied the suggestion. You could have said, "No! I won't indulge in vengeful thoughts. Christ forgave me for my sins, and now I'm going to forgive that man." After that you would need to get your heart and mind on another track, such as praying and reciting Bible verses to yourself. It isn't easy, but you *can* avoid sinning.

Temptation Doesn't Involve Guilt; Sin Does

Have you ever said to yourself, "I must be way out of fellowship with God because of all the filthy thoughts that enter my mind"? That's another of Satan's outrageous lies. He wants us to think that just because we're tempted, we've let God down. And that's not true.

The experience of Jesus proves it. Hebrews 4:15 teaches that He was "tempted in all things as *we are, yet* without sin." Whatever temptation you might experience, your Lord experienced it, too. Yet He never sinned! Nothing could be clearer than that in Hebrews 4:15. So we don't need to feel guilty just because we're tempted. This is where I've seen many believers lose their joy and become discouraged. Don't let it happen to you. Only when we yield to temptation do we incur guilt.

Temptation Is Inevitable; But Sin Doesn't Have to Follow It

If Jesus had to be tempted, you and I must accept our share of it, too. There's no escape from temptations or suggestions to sin. But that doesn't mean we have to yield to them. Oscar Wilde, the famed playwright, once said, "I can resist anything but temptation."[1] We may smile at that, but for the believer in Christ that statement is not true. Many times I've listened to Christians who have confessed, "I can't help but give in to this certain temptation in my life."

That's exactly how your spiritual enemy wants you to feel. But listen to this promise from 1 Corinthians 10:13. "God...with the temptation will provide the way of escape also, that you may be able to endure it."

Evening always follows afternoon, but sin doesn't have to follow temptation. This can be true in our lives because our heavenly Father has armed us with two tremendous weapons to overcome temptation. They are the same two powers Jesus employed when the devil tempted Him. You can read the accounts in Matthew 4:1-11 and Luke 4:1-13.

First, Christ withstood Satan's temptations because *He was filled with the Scriptures*. The devil launched three major attacks against our Lord. And all three times Jesus defended Himself by quoting passages from the Bible. When He said, "It is written," Satan was immediately cut down. The devil had no arguments, rebuttals, or plea bargains. The only thing the enemy could do was back off and try another line of approach.

Jesus' example teaches us that the Bible is a great weapon against temptation. Ephesians 6:17 speaks of "the sword of the Spirit, which is the word of God." Count on this: The better you know your Bible, the greater the victory you'll enjoy over sin in your life.

Psalm 119:11 puts it this way: "Thy word I have treasured in my heart, that I may not sin against Thee." That verse encourages us to memorize portions of Scripture. Jesus certainly did. When tempted by Satan in the desert, He had no access to scrolls of Old Testament Scripture. He recited verses that He had committed to memory.

You've noticed at the end of each chapter in this book there is a verse or more to memorize. You need them! In a personal letter to me, one of our church members looked back on her early days in Christ and testified, "I was assailed by Satan with doubts. I struggled with this for months. It wasn't until I began memorizing Scripture that the doubts stopped."

By the time I was five years old, my mother had encouraged and assisted me in memorizing several dozen Bible verses. Over the years I've committed many more to memory, and I can bear witness that often they have kept me out of sin. Try it for yourself. Memorization is a great way to be filled with the Scriptures, and I promise you'll be stronger.

Second, Christ won the victory over temptation because *He was filled with the Spirit.* Luke's account of the battle with Satan makes it clear that Jesus was full of the Holy Spirit's power before, during, and after His temptations (Luke 4:1,14). That's the same Holy Spirit who lives inside you! As you submit yourself to His indwelling power, He'll help you say no to the tempter's voice.

Christians who feel powerless against temptation often despair. But that feeling should lead them to the "secret of success." The secret lies in the fact that the real problem with many of us is not that we're too weak, but that we're too strong! We're just strong enough to fight off some temptations in our own strength. But then we rely on human power to resist all enticements,

It's encouraging to know that Jesus used the same two weapons—Scripture and the Holy Spirit—against temptation, the same weapons that are available to us today.

and that never works. We need to understand our total weakness. Only then will we depend on God's Spirit for the victory. That is the "secret to success"!

Isn't it encouraging to know that Jesus used the same two weapons—Scripture and the Holy Spirit—against temptation, the same weapons that are available to us today? So let's follow His example seriously and use the Bible and the Spirit in our struggle against temptation.

Temptations Are Necessary; Sin Isn't

You may be surprised to hear that temptations are necessary, but it's true. First Peter 1:6 says, "If necessary, you have been distressed by various trials." The Greek word for *trials* is translated "temptations" elsewhere in the New Testament. So we could render it that way here. Also, Jesus Himself declared in Matthew 18:7: "It is necessary that temptations come" (*RSV*). We will now discover why they are necessary.

Hebrews 2:18 tells us that Jesus "suffered" through His temptations. A bit later it says, "Although He was a Son, He learned obedience from the things which He suffered" (Hebrews 5:8). By putting those two verses together, we see that even our Lord learned from His temptations. They actually benefited Him!

And they help us, too. Temptations stretch our spiritual muscles. They drive us to prayer. They keep us from growing proud. They make us long for heaven. And they build in us compassion for others who are also struggling. So, yes, temptations are necessary.

But sin isn't. Have you ever heard a Christian share how God rescued him from sexual sin, drug addiction, or alcoholism? Those testimonies are impressive. But they often make listeners sigh and say, "I wish I had a testimony like that." No one, however, needs to experience sin. Sin only tears down, hinders fellowship with

Christ, and ruins one's testimony. It never helps anyone, especially a Christian.

Previously, I stated that temptations are necessary. But I must add that you shouldn't go looking for them. Believe me, you'll encounter enough suggestions without inviting more.

When it comes to the four distinctions between temptation and sin that are discussed in this chapter, be assured that the devil is delighted to confuse you. However, it is God's desire that you be not ignorant of Satan's schemes (2 Corinthians 2:11).

What you must know to grow:

There is a vast difference between temptation and sin. Jesus Himself was tempted in every way as you are, yet He never sinned. You can experience victory over temptation, because God always provides a way of escape!

Simple-to-follow steps for Christian growth:

- Make use of the two weapons the Lord offers you—the Scriptures and the Holy Spirit.
- The Bible will give you wisdom to see through Satan's schemes. Read it, study it, and commit parts of it to memory.
- The Holy Spirit will supply you with supernatural power to fight off temptation. So surrender yourself to His control.
- Memorize 1 Corinthians 10:13.

Ten

Why Do My Prayers Seem to Bounce Off the Ceiling?

Call to Me, and I will answer you,
and I will tell you great and mighty things,
which you do not know.
Jeremiah 33:3

Prayer has been described as the autograph of the Holy Spirit on the heart of every believer. Yet most Christians struggle with it. Many feel frustrated, as if their prayers are bouncing off the ceiling.

In this chapter, I want to give you six reasons why your prayers might be doing just that. Think of these reasons as six traps to avoid in your prayer life.

Reason #1: Vague Requests

Philippians 4:6 holds out this invitation: "Let your requests be made known to God." Are you suffering from a disease and want to be healed? Do you yearn to see your spouse become a Christian? Are you waiting for a new job? Whatever it is, "Let your requests be made known to God"!

That admonition means that prayer should be specific. People who came to Jesus in the New Testament didn't recite prayers to Him. They simply unburdened their hearts. That's what God wants us to do. Often I hear Christians pray like this: "Dear God, I pray for Joe in the hospital. And bless Susan's marriage. And I pray for Linda's son."

That kind of prayer is better than nothing, but it's too vague! The same prayer, made specific, might sound like this: "Dear God, fill Joe's heart with peace as he anticipates his cancer surgery tomorrow. Grant Susan a persevering spirit while she waits for her husband to accept Christ. And give Linda's son the courage to say no to the boys at school who are trying to sell him drugs."

That's more specific. Imagine a marksman shooting his rifle at random in every direction. He's not going to hit the target very often. So it is with prayer that isn't clearly expressed. It fails for lack of direction. Our heavenly Father wants us to be focused in our prayers.

Reason #2: Unclaimed Scriptural Promises

When a person writes you a check, you endorse it, take it to the bank, and cash it. Do the same with prayer.

Think of the Bible's promises as checks our heavenly Father makes out to you. First, endorse the promise by believing it's true, and not just true in general, but true for you. Second, lay that promise out before the Lord in prayer, just like you'd present a check to the teller at a bank. Finally, because this is a promise given in the Word of God, and therefore trustworthy, receive it as a part of your experience.

Here's an example. In James 1:5-8 the Bible promises that if we lack wisdom, we can ask God for it, and He'll give it to us. Suppose you sense a need for wisdom to counsel a friend who is depressed and turning to you for help. You read James 1:5-8 and exercise faith that it's a promise for you in your situation. In that way you endorse the check.

Then you bow before God and pray, "Heavenly Father, You said that if I required wisdom, You'd give it to me. I do need it—to help Jane through her depression. Please fulfill this promise in my life. I choose to believe that the proper wisdom will be mine. Thank You, in Jesus' name. Amen."

That prayer is the Christian's way of taking the scriptural check to the bank and cashing it! Of course, the Bible is filled with many other promises to claim. I've only used one example. You're going to discover many more as you get into God's Word.

If you want to pattern your prayer life after the Master's, intercede for other people.

Reason #3: Selfishness

I heard about a man who bowed his head and prayed, "God bless me, my wife, and my two children—us four, and no more, forevermore. Amen."

I don't know if that story is true or not, but it makes a good point. That man's prayer betrayed a selfish attitude. Our Lord wants us to pray for others, not just for ourselves. The word for this is *intercession*. It's probably the highest form of prayer.

Perhaps you're wondering, "For whom should I pray, besides my family members?"

How about praying for people who do not know Christ as their Savior? And for your pastor and other spiritual leaders? For missionaries your church supports and people involved in ministries you're familiar with outside the church, leaders in government, the sick, the elderly, shut-ins? For those with special needs, such as job interviews, exams in school, the loss of a spouse through death or divorce, and for people who have problem children? And these suggestions are just for starters. Many times in your Christian life you will discover that other believers will share a request with you and ask you to pray for them.

Although you may find it difficult to talk to non-believers about Christ, you can be encouraged in the knowledge that you can talk to Christ about them. And the more you mention *them* to your Lord, the easier you'll find it to mention *Him* to them.

When Christ was on earth, much of His prayer life was spent in intercession. Sometimes He even prayed for His enemies! In fact, as soon as they nailed Him to the cross, He prayed, "Father, forgive them" (Luke 23:34).

Since Christ's ascension into heaven, He hasn't ceased to pray for us. Hebrews 7:25 says, "He always lives to make intercession" for us. If you want to pattern your prayer life after the Master's, intercede for other people. God will honor you for it.

Reason #4: Failure to Live in an Attitude of Prayer

One of the shortest verses in the Bible commands us to "pray without ceasing" (1 Thessalonians 5:17). Sounds impossible, doesn't it? How can we pray non-stop? Obviously, we can't always be down on our knees with heads bowed and eyes closed, praying. This verse is talking about living in an attitude of prayer. God wants us always to be in touch with Him. There should never be a time in our daily schedule when prayer would mean an abrupt change of pace for us, because we're already living in the spirit of prayer.

Suppose you're driving a car on a 200-mile trip. All afternoon you're listening to the radio, enjoying the scenery, and talking with a passenger in the car. Once you arrive at your destination, you can hardly recall the many turns you made on the road, the number of times you put your foot on the brake or accelerator, and your changing of lanes on the highway. You made all those driving operations almost subconsciously. And yet they were the controlling factors of the trip.

So it is with prayer. While we're busy working, interacting with people, spending time with our families, and enjoying our hobbies, God wants us to undergird everything with a spirit of prayer that controls our thoughts, words, and actions. And when the time comes for a more conscious, deliberate prayer, the transition will be natural.

Reason #5: Doubt that God Will Answer

Martin Luther once said, "We must not think of prayer

as overcoming God's reluctance, but as laying hold of His highest willingness."

A woman was in desperate need of $337 to pay her overdue utility bill. So she went to her knees and asked the Lord for it. An hour later the mailman delivered a tax-refund check from the Internal Revenue Service for exactly $337! She lifted her eyes toward heaven and said, "Lord, remember that prayer request I made for $337? Never mind. Someone else provided it!"

She didn't expect God to answer and was, therefore, blind to the answer when it came.

Shortly after leading a friend of mine to Christ, I joined with him in a specific prayer request. When the Lord granted it a few days later, I remarked to the new Christian, "It's a miracle!"

With a confused look on his face, he replied, "Isn't that the business God is in?"

Yes, it is! And how pleased I was to see expectant faith in my friend's heart. New Christians can sometimes teach even their pastors a needed lesson.

Reason #6: Resistance to God's Will

The Lord is pleased to answer prayer, but not always our way. Not everything you ask for will be granted. Remember, the Bible only invites us to let our *requests* be made known to God, not our *demands*.

Earlier I said that you could claim God's promises in the Bible. But there are some situations in life for which there is no specific promise to claim. The heavenly Father never obligates Himself in Scripture to give us the job we think we need, the person we choose for a marriage partner, or perfect health that we are convinced is necessary. If you have a desire in those areas, let it be known to God. But don't become bitter if He overrules your request.

The night before He died, Jesus asked His Father to spare Him the suffering of the cross, but God answered no. Our Lord could rest content in that, because He had added these words to His request: "Yet not My will, but Thine be done" (Luke 22:42).

The Apostle Paul begged the Lord three times to remove his painful "thorn in the flesh." But all three times God answered no. He wanted Paul to learn the value of His all-sufficient grace (2 Corinthians 12:7-10).

Now if Jesus and Paul had to pray in submission to God's will, surely we do, too.

An unknown Confederate soldier who wrote the following words shows us how denials of our requests can be God's richest yes:

I asked the Lord for strength, that I might achieve;
   I was made weak, that I might learn humbly to
      obey.
I asked for health, that I might do greater things;
   I was given infirmity, that I might do better
      things.
I asked for riches, that I might be happy;
   I was given poverty, that I might be wise.
I asked for power, that I might have the praise
      of men;
   I was given weakness, that I might feel the need
      of God.
I asked for all things, that I might enjoy life;
   I was given life, that I might enjoy all things.
I got nothing that I asked for—
   but everything I had hoped for.
Almost despite myself,
   my unspoken prayers were answered.
I am among all men most richly blessed.[1]

What you must know to grow:

Prayer is communication with God and therefore vital to your Christian growth. This is a fulfilling, rewarding discipline. But it's also hard work! If you don't know how to pray, you'll feel like you're only talking to yourself.

Simple-to-follow steps for Christian growth:

- Pray specifically, claiming the Bible's promises.
- Intercede for others.
- Live in an attitude of prayer.
- Expect God to answer.
- Submit to His will.
- Memorize Jeremiah 33:3.

Note:
1. *Hymns for the Family of God* (Nashville, TN: Paragon Associates, 1976), p. 527.

Eleven

I Can Worship God at the Beach...Can't I?

And let us consider
how to stimulate one another
to love and good deeds,
not forsaking our own assembling together,
Hebrews 10:24-25

It's been said that a church is made up of four kinds of people: *wishbones* who spend all their time wishing someone else would do the work; *jawbones* who do all the talking but little else; *knucklebones* who knock everything everyone else does; and *backbones* who carry the load and complete the work. I think we can add a fifth group: *broken bones*—people who belong to Christ but aren't active in His church.

"But I don't have to go to church to be a Christian," many have said. "I can worship God at the beach... can't I?"

Yes, you can. I like to compare the church to a bus station. It doesn't take you to your destination (heaven), but it's a good place to meet the bus (Jesus Christ) that will! Just as you can board a bus somewhere on the road, so you can meet the Lord Jesus in a home, at work, school, or anywhere else. But a bus station is the normal place to get on a bus. In the same way, the church is a likely place to be introduced to Christ.

Whereas attending church isn't a ticket to heaven, it is a training ground for it. Once Jesus saves us, the church nurtures us in the faith. Yes, you can be a Christian without attending church. But it's something like being a student who doesn't attend classes, an athlete who doesn't show up for practice, or a soldier who is absent without leave. Surely if our faith is strong enough to get us into heaven, it should be strong enough to take us to church. God's Word even commands us not to neglect the regular meetings of the church (Hebrews 10:25, *TLB*).

What Is the Church?

The English word *church* comes from a Greek term that means "the Lord's." You can see that for yourself in an English dictionary. The church, then, is the cherished possession of Jesus Christ. The first time the word occurs in the Bible, Jesus calls it "My church" (Matthew 16:18). He values it highly—and so should we.

The New Testament uses four metaphors to describe the church. First, it is the *body of Christ* (1 Corinthians 12:27; Ephesians 1:22-23; Colossians 1:18,24). Jesus is the head, and we're the bodily parts—the fingers, toes, joints, and muscles. Now suppose I'm a finger, but I'm not active in the church. Then to all appearances Jesus Christ has only three fingers and a thumb on His hand. As far as the world can see, Christ is mutilated by my absence from the body. Not only that, but a finger needs the rest of the body to survive. It wasn't made for isolation.

Second, the church is called the *bride of Christ* (2 Corinthians 11:2; Ephesians 5:22-33; Revelation 19:7-8). That means He loves her! Jesus looks upon His church as a groom views his bride marching up the aisle to him on their wedding day. Since our Lord loves the church, we should, too.

Third, the church is described as the *branches of Christ* (John 15:1-8). The branches are where the fruit is produced. So if we want to be productive Christians, we should be active in the church. Again, this isn't to say the church is the only place where you can bear spiritual fruit. But it's a likely place.

Fourth, the church is sometimes pictured as the *building of Christ* (1 Corinthians 3:16; Ephesians 2:19-22; 1 Peter 2:4-5). A building is a place where

Don't look for a perfect church. There's no such thing!

someone lives and works. So Christ lives in His church and works through it. It's meant to be our spiritual home and place of service, too.

The importance of the church can also be seen in the New Testament metaphors for individual Christians. We're sheep who need to stay together in one flock (Luke 15:4-6), brothers and sisters who belong to the same household (1 Corinthians 8:12-13), soldiers who are active in God's army (2 Timothy 2:3), citizens who make up one kingdom (Philippians 3:20), and priests who serve in the same temple (1 Peter 2:5). These illustrations reveal that God didn't create us to live by ourselves. He wants us together!

What Kind of Church Should You Attend?

Let me point out some distinctions you should look for when seeking a church. First, look for a *Christ-centered* church that focuses on worshiping the Lord Jesus, not on entertaining the people. In a Christ-centered church, when you leave the sanctuary, there'll be no doubt that Christ was the center of attention. He was adored, praised, preached, prayed to, sung to, and sung about. And not merely as a good Teacher or moral example, but as the crucified Savior and living Lord.

Second, look for a church that *emphasizes the new birth in Christ*. This doesn't mean it must have public invitations to accept Jesus at the end of each worship service. But the message should be clear that people need to be made new in Christ. I've talked with numerous men and women who have attended church for years and have never learned the necessity of a conversion experience. How tragic! If the church's basic message is "Try to live your best, and God will be pleased," such a church has lost its spiritual identity.

Third, look for a church that *teaches and preaches the Word of God*. The sermons and classes should be full of biblical instruction. This will feed your heart, give you wisdom, train you in godliness, and help you grow.

Fourth, look for a *loving* church. Jesus said, "By this all men will know that you are My disciples, if you have love for one another" (John 13:35). I've heard many people say they knew a certain church was right for them as soon as they walked through the door; love was the telltale sign. In a congregation like that, "outsiders" easily become "insiders."

Fifth, look for a church with a *sense of mission*. Jesus commanded us to make disciples of all nations (Matthew 28:19-20). We call that passage "The Great Commission." The church should be outreaching, yet many are ingrown. They gather for their holy huddle on Sundays, completely indifferent to the needs of the world. They're in a maintenance mode. A church, just like an individual believer, should always be growing. If a congregation is satisfied to nurture itself without seeking to win lost people to Jesus Christ, it has neglected its marching orders.

Finally, don't look for a perfect church. There's no such thing!

When you find a good place of worship, give it your best. Introduce yourself to the pastor. Pray for him regularly and encourage him. If the church has a formal membership, join it. If it has Sunday evening worship services, attend them. Get involved in a church school or Sunday School class. It's a great place to learn and discuss God's Word and enjoy fellowship with others in a group setting. Most churches also offer home Bible study groups during the week. They are a tremendous source of spiritual growth. And support your church financially, remembering that you're giving to Christ when you give to His church. Also keep in mind that the church is there not only to serve you, but to be a channel through which you may serve the Lord and people in need.

If you receive these suggestions and put them into practice, you'll be part of the *backbone* of your church. Your church will grow, and so will you!

What you must know to grow:

Jesus Christ Himself created the church. He loves it as His prized possession. He has chosen to work through it. No child of God should despise or neglect it.

Simple-to-follow steps for Christian growth:

- Become involved in a Christ-centered, evangelistic, Bible-based, loving, outreaching church "on the grow."
- Get to know its pastor and people.
- Support the church with your prayers, service, and finances.
- Memorize Hebrews 10:24-25.

Twelve

Do I Have to Be Committed?

I urge you therefore, brethren, by the mercies of God,
to present your bodies a living
and holy sacrifice, acceptable to God,
which is your spiritual service of worship.

Romans 12:1

In the nineteenth century, British evangelist Henry Varley remarked to Dwight L. Moody, "It remains to be seen what God will do with a man who gives himself up wholly to Him."

Those words made a deep impression on Moody. He replied to Mr. Varley, "Well, I will be that man!"[1]

And he was! He went on to become the most famous evangelist of the nineteenth century. Church historians tell us that Moody preached to more than 100-million people in his ministry.[2] Eternity alone will reveal how many of them found the Savior.

Okay, so you'll probably never be another Dwight L. Moody. But I tell his story to remind you that commitment makes the difference in every Christian's life.

Do I have to be committed? you ask. That depends. Do you want to grow? Do you want your life to count for Christ? Do you want to glorify God?

Jesus said that anyone who desires to follow Him must "take up his cross daily" (Luke 9:23). In the first century, the cross was used for one thing—killing people. It was an instrument of death. Jesus Himself was executed on one (John 19:16-19). Therefore, to take up your cross as a follower of Christ means you're willing to die for Him. That's commitment! Our Lord wants us to be willing to go to the limit for Him.

You might be thinking, *But I already made a commitment to Jesus when I became a Christian.*

True. But even believers need to renew their dedication. The Apostle Paul challenged the Christians in

Rome with these words: "I urge you therefore, brethren, by the mercies of God, to present your bodies a living and holy sacrifice, acceptable to God, which is your spiritual service of worship" (Romans 12:1).

What Difference Does It Make?

Your choice to obey or disobey the challenge to present your body a living sacrifice will dictate many things in your spiritual life. If you commit yourself unconditionally to the Lord, you'll be joyful, strong, useful to God, walking with Christ, and victorious over sin. But if you refuse to give yourself in dedication, it will lead to unhappiness, frustration, loss of fellowship with the Lord, and spiritual defeat.

A committed Christian lives for Jesus; an uncommitted one lives for himself. A committed Christian is self-disciplined to spend time alone with God every day in Scripture and prayer; an uncommitted one lacks that kind of discipline, and it shows in his life. A committed Christian makes a difference in other people's lives; so does an uncommitted one, but instead of building others up, he becomes a stumbling block to them. A committed Christian grows in faith, knowledge, and love; an uncommitted one sinks into doubts, needless ignorance, and a feeling of indifference.

Philip Henry was the father of Matthew Henry, who wrote a famous commentary on the Bible. When his children were about to be baptized, Philip composed a pledge of commitment for them. Each one recited it as a profession of his or her personal dedication to Christ. Here it is:

I take God to be my chief end and highest good.
I take the Son of God to be my Prince and Savior.
I take the Spirit of God to be my Sanctifier, Teacher,
    Guide, and Comforter.

God delights to work through people who surrender totally to His Son.

I take the Word of God to be my rule in all my actions.
I take the people of God to be my people under all
    conditions.
I do hereby dedicate and devote to the Lord
  all I am,
  all I have,
  and all I can do.
I make this commitment
  deliberately,
    freely,
      and forever.

I recommend that pledge of commitment to you. Write
it down. Put it in a prominent place—maybe on your
refrigerator, your desk, the dashboard of your car, or the
inside cover of your Bible. Keep it always before you.
More importantly, live it out. And God will use you. You'll
be a Christian on the grow!

What you must know to grow:

Commitment makes all the difference in your spiritual growth. God delights to work through people who
surrender totally to His Son.

Simple-to-follow steps for Christian growth:

● Make a solemn vow that Christ will always have first
place in your life.
● Pledge to be obedient to the Word of God, submissive
to the will of God, and involved in the work of God—
nothing less, nothing else, at any cost!
● Memorize Romans 12:1-2.

Notes:

1. R. A. Torrey, "Why God Used D. L. Moody," *Sword of the Lord* magazine (February 27, 1981), p. 1.
2. Bruce L. Shelley (J. D. Douglas, General Editor), *The New International Dictionary of the Christian Church* (Grand Rapids, MI: Zondervan, 1974), p. 675.

A One-Year Plan for Bible Verse Memorization

The following is a list of thirty-nine Bible verses I recommend that you commit to memory during the coming year. All the verses assigned at the conclusion of the chapters in this book are contained in this list.

If you memorize one verse each week for three weeks and then spend the fourth week in review, you'll learn all thirty-nine verses in one year! Place a check mark on the line in the right-hand column when you have memorized the verse or completed your review.

The Plan of Salvation

Week 1:	Romans 8:1	_____
Week 2:	John 1:12	_____
Week 3:	John 3:16	_____
Week 4:	Review	_____
Week 5:	John 14:6	_____
Week 6:	Romans 3:23	_____
Week 7:	Romans 5:8	_____
Week 8:	Review	_____
Week 9:	Romans 6:23	_____
Week 10:	Romans 10:9	_____
Week 11:	1 John 1:9	_____
Week 12:	Review	_____
Week 13:	Ephesians 2:8	_____
Week 14:	Ephesians 2:9	_____
Week 15:	2 Corinthians 5:17	_____
Week 16:	Review	_____

Assurance of Salvation

Week 17:	1 John 5:11	_____
Week 18:	1 John 5:12	_____
Week 19:	1 John 5:13	_____

Week 20:   Review   _____
Week 21:   Revelation 3:20   _____

The Bible

Week 22:   Psalm 119:11   _____
Week 23:   Psalm 119:105   _____
Week 24:   Review   _____
Week 25:   2 Timothy 3:16   _____
Week 26:   2 Timothy 3:17   _____

Temptation

Week 27:   1 Corinthians 10:13   _____
Week 28:   Review   _____

Prayer

Week 29:   Jeremiah 33:3   _____
Week 30:   Matthew 7:7   _____

Witnessing

Week 31:   Acts 1:8   _____
Week 32:   Review   _____
Week 33:   Matthew 28:19   _____
Week 34:   Matthew 28:20   _____

Christian Living

Week 35:   Matthew 6:33   _____
Week 36:   Review   _____
Week 37:   Romans 12:1   _____
Week 38:   Romans 12:2   _____
Week 39:   Philippians 4:13   _____
Week 40:   Review   _____
Week 41:   Galatians 2:20   _____

The Church

Week 42:	Hebrews 10:24	_____
Week 43:	Hebrews 10:25	_____
Week 44:	Review	_____

The Holy Spirit

Week 45:	1 Corinthians 6:19	_____
Week 46:	1 Corinthians 6:20	_____
Week 47:	Galatians 5:22	_____
Week 48:	Review	_____
Week 49:	Galatians 5:23	_____

The Second Coming of Christ

Week 50:	1 Thessalonians 4:16	_____
Week 51:	1 Thessalonians 4:17	_____
Week 52:	Review	_____